ULTIMATE
FIELD TRIP 3

WADING INTO MARINE BIOLOGY

by Susan E. Goodman   photographs by Michael J. Doolittle

Aladdin Paperbacks

First Aladdin Paperbacks edition September 2000

ALADDIN PAPERBACKS
An imprint of Simon & Schuster Children's Publishing Division
1230 Avenue of the Americas
New York, NY 10020

Also available in an Atheneum Books for Young Readers hardcover edition.

Book design by Anne Scatto/PIXEL PRESS
The text of this book is set in Monotype Fournier.

Printed and bound in Hong Kong
10 9 8 7 6 5 4 3 2 1

The Library of Congress has catalogued the hardcover edition as follows:
Goodman, Susan E., 1952-
Ultimate Field Trip 3: Wading into marine biology / by Susan E. Goodman; photographs by Michael J. Doolittle.—1st ed.
p. cm. "An ultimate field trip."
Includes bibliographical references (p.)
Summary: A middle-school class from Boston visits Cobscook Bay, Maine, to learn
about the marine biology of the bay's tidal zones.
ISBN: 0-689-81963-3
1. Tide pool ecology—Study and teaching (Elementary)—
Maine—Cobscook Bay—Juvenile literature. 2. Tide pools—
Study and teaching (Elementary)—Maine—Cobscook
Bay—Juvenile Literature. 3. Marine biology—
Study and teaching (Elementary)—Maine—Cobscook
Bay—Juvenile literature. [1. Tide pool ecology. 2. Tide
pools. 3. Ecology. 4. Marine biology. 5. Cobscook Bay
(Me.) 6. School field trips.]
I. Doolittle, Michael J., ill. II. Title.
QH105.M2G58 1999 577.69'9—dc21
98-13985
ISBN 0-689-83890-5 (Aladdin paperback)

To Mike, the best collaborator a writer could have.
—S. C.

To Grandpa D, who devoted most of his life to middle-school kids.
—M. D.

First we'd like to thank the kids attending this program and Brent Jackson of the Museum of Science, who graciously invited us along and eased our way through the trip. Thanks to everyone at Friedman Field Station, especially Chery Gibson, Jennifer Kelly, Paul Ellingwood, Christiana Soares, Lila Austin, Ralph and Malachi Moody— and Dr. Carl Merrill, for all his time and his expert review of the manuscript. Deborah Hirschland was a warm, insightful reader, and, at Atheneum, Howard Kaplan helped with endless details. As always, Marcia Marshall has been a great editor and friend.

CONTENTS

AT RIGHT: Our group of tidal zone explorers. Standing from left to right: Ben Bakker, Richard Balouskus, Vladimir Skaletsky, Gregory Kierstead, Kendra Mariassy, Jennifer Cohuru, Sedrine Caterson, Nicole Syngajewski. Middle row from left to right: Bill Hall, Roger Centeio, Mary Kilgoe, Paul Buckley, Laila Taylor, Mary Humphrey, Matt Goodridge. Front row from left to right: Jennifer Babineau, Amie Hopkins, Katelyn McLaughlin, Rand Niederhoffer, Alexa Meehan, Hannah Nelson, Andrew Roy.

CHAPTER 1

LIFE in the TIDAL ZONE

Imagine living in a world that changes every six hours. First it sits underwater, then in open air. The temperature jumps from cold to steaming within minutes and from cool to freezing just as quickly. This world can be calm. And it can be battered by walls of water crashing down at twenty-five miles an hour.

This is the tidal zone—land covered and uncovered by the ocean as the tide

climbs up and down the shore. To survive, the plants and animals of the tidal zone must be able to adjust to many different conditions. Snails creep along, for example, until the waves roll in. Then they attach themselves to rocks, using their single foot like a suction cup. Barnacles also avoid being swept out to sea by cementing themselves to rocks. Then, when the tide retreats, these barnacles close their shells tight to keep their wet world safely inside. Clams dig into the sand and wait for the water's return.

Every beach has a tidal zone, but the one in Cobscook Bay, Maine, is special. Its tides are among the highest in the world. In some places, the water climbs a mile onto shore. The bay's tidal zone is so big that the plants and animals living at its top are completely different from the ones closest to the ocean. Many marine biologists, scientists who study life in and around the sea, come to Cobscook Bay to learn how its creatures adapt to such a complicated life.

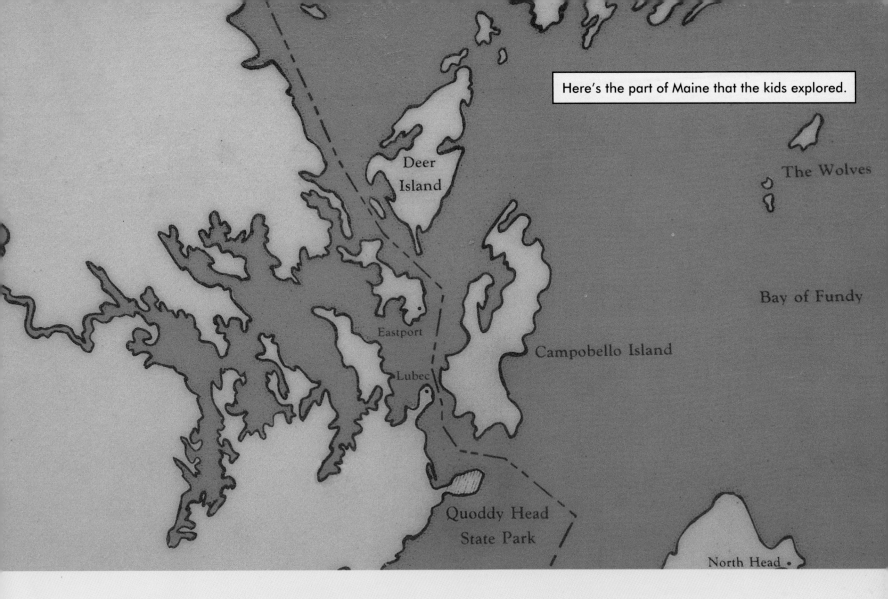

Here's the part of Maine that the kids explored.

Deer Island

The Wolves

Bay of Fundy

Eastport

Campobello Island

Lubec

Quoddy Head
State Park

North Head

And they aren't alone. A group of middle-school kids came up to Suffolk University's Friedman Field Station. During their one-week program, they braved cold water and crab claws, searched for rock eels, and sailed the ocean to explore this amazing world.

CHAPTER 2

MEETING the TIDAL RESIDENTS

A good way to learn about the tidal zone is to meet the animals that live there. On their first day in Maine, the kids put on their old sneakers or rubber boots. They were off to the bay for a look at its tidal residents—up close and personal.

"Soon it will be low tide, when the water's at its lowest point on the shore. That's the best time to find specimens," announced Dr. Carl Merrill, the marine biologist in charge of the field station. "In fact, we'd better get going; we don't have that much time. Our tide comes back in fast, about one vertical foot every fifteen minutes."

"In other words, the tide climbs from your foot to your calf in about fifteen minutes," explained Chery Gibson, another instructor. "But since most beaches are set at an angle, the water could travel three, four feet up the shore in that same amount of time.

"The first time I was here, somebody asked me a question," Chery continued. "I needed my hands to answer, so I put my camera in a bucket beside me on the beach. By the time I'd finished, the bucket had already started floating and tipped over. My camera was ruined, but I learned to respect the tides."

"Wow," said Ben, "can they be dangerous?"

"You have to be careful," said Carl. "I've heard of plenty of hikers whose paths home were covered by water. Here, our rule is you don't go by the bay unless you're with a counselor. Another rule—after you've looked at a specimen, put it back exactly where you found it. Placing it just a few feet away could put it into another environment where it might not survive."

"While you're looking at something, try to notice how it has adapted to its place in the tidal zone," said Chery. "How

A type of sea star called a sun star typically has eight to twelve legs, but when Paul first saw it, he asked, "Is this a radioactive mutant?"

"They are gripping on my fingers," said Jen B. "I'm the Starfish Queen!"

11

does it stay wet during low tide? How does it avoid being eaten? What makes this animal special?"

Lugging their buckets, the kids tramped down to a part of the bay called the Narrows. Before he set them loose, Carl put a thermometer in the water. "Right now the water is about sixty-four degrees, a bit warmer than at high tide," he said. "It has heated up while sitting on shore."

"You call this warm?" Amie said as she waded in.

"No problem, I'm wearing two pairs of socks inside my boots," said Bill. "But my feet are so smooshed, I feel like one of those old Chinese women."

Soon, however, the kids forgot about their cold feet and goose bumps.

"Mussels by the millions!" said Kendra.

"Here's a whole city of them," said Roger. "They're crunching under my feet."

"They certainly couldn't get

ABOVE: Green crabs thrive on Maine's coast, but they're not a native species. They may have accidentally immigrated to America with early European settlers.

AT RIGHT: "This seaweed looks like plastic wrap and feels like it too," said Sedrine.

out of your way," said Chery, as they kneeled for a closer look. "Mussels tie themselves to rocks and seaweed using strings they make called byssal threads. That way, waves can't carry them out to sea. If you were stuck in one place like these mussels, how could you get your food?"

"Take-out?" Katelyn said, laughing.

"Try filtration," said Chery. "When it's covered with water, the mussel opens its shell. As water flows past its mouth, the mussel filters out tiny one-celled creatures and eats them."

"I found an eel," Rand shouted as she lifted a rock. "Will it bite me?"

"I got one too," said Matt. "It feels so funny in your hand."

Rock gunnels hide in crevices and under rocks and seaweed. They are also called "butterfish" because they're so hard to catch.

"It squirms like an eel, so people call it a 'rock eel,'" explained an instructor named Jennifer Kelly. "Actually, it's a fish called a rock gunnel. And don't worry, Rand, it eats shrimp and worms—not kids."

"Carl said they can't live out of water very long," said Richard. "We better put them back under their rocks."

At 1:45 P.M., Carl announced, "The current has stopped going out. Notice how still the water is. In just a minute, it will start coming back in."

The kids paused, but just for a moment. They were much more interested in their treasure hunt.

"I just found some mussels all together in a group," said Greg. "I wonder if they stick together for safety."

"Chery, check out this huge shell," said Hannah.

"That belonged to a moon snail, a fierce predator," said Chery. "Have you ever seen shells with a hole in them?"

"Aren't those holes there so you can make necklaces?" joked Laila.

"The moon snail holds a clam down with its foot and uses its radula, or tongue, to drill a hole in the shell," Chery explained. "Then it sucks the clam out and eats it."

"Starfish!" said Nicole, as she turned a common sea star over to examine its underside. "Look at all those little things. Are they teeth?"

"They're tube feet," said Carl. Then he explained how the starfish, or sea star, walks by pumping those tubes full of water and attaching the little suction cups at their tips onto something solid. When the sea star lets the water out, its feet recoil, pulling the animal forward.

At 2:03 P.M., Chery told the kids to watch the current. "The water's really coming in now," she said.

Carl placed his thermometer in the water. "The water coming in from the ocean is colder," he said. "The temperature has already dropped to sixty-one degrees."

There's more than one way to rinse off mud and seawater.

"Start back in," Chery called to the group who had walked across low-tide mud to a nearby island. "I don't want to have to get you in the boat."

A few minutes later, Mary K. was looking for sea stars. "Hey, I'm sinking," she said.

"No you aren't," Amie replied, "the water's rising."

"That's cool!" Nicole exclaimed.

"No, it's scary," said Mary K. Then she pretended she was the Wicked Witch of the West and shrieked, "I'm melting!"

The tide was covering their hunting grounds; it was time to leave. As she walked back, Mary H. said, "We're stepping on so many little mussels."

"I know," said Laila. "Every time I feel a crunch, I feel guilty now."

"I hate to think about what's in my shoe," said Hannah.

"I call the first shower," shouted Greg.

"Not if I get there before you!" Ben replied.

How Tides Work

The distance high tide climbs onto the shore changes over the course of a month. Since each high tide marks the shore by leaving debris, this picture shows a part of the cycle when the high tides are getting lower.

Long ago, people thought tides rose and fell as a sea god swallowed and spit out water. The real cause is up in space, not down at the bottom of the sea. The moon's gravity acts like a magnet pulling the earth's oceans. So the water level in the ocean closest to the moon rises up into high tide. At the same time, the water on the opposite side of Earth rides high as well. Meanwhile, the rest of Earth's oceans sink to a lower level. Since Earth rotates, the moon's pull upon the oceans moves across the globe. Most spots have two high tides and two low tides just about every day.

All beaches have tides, but the ones at Cobscook Bay are special. Cobscook Bay is part of the Bay of Fundy, which has the highest tides in the world. Most other bays have shallow, sloping sides, but this bay is steep-sided like a bath-tub. When water rushes from the wide ocean into this narrow, steep place, there's no-where to go but up. In some places, the difference between high and low tide can be as much as forty-eight vertical feet, the height of a four-story build-ing!

Here's Katelyn standing on the shore at 4:05 P.M. . . .

. . . and in the same spot forty-five minutes later.

CHAPTER 3

ANALYZING RACCOON BEACH

Tidal zones come in all sorts of packages. The kids saw a protected beach inside the bay the day they collected specimens at the Narrows. Raccoon Beach, exposed to open ocean, was a very different environment.

"It's pretty calm now," Carl told the kids as they headed down the shore. "But when the waves are crashing down in winter, you can hear rocks the size of your head being tossed around."

Raccoon Beach was so rugged, the kids easily understood why animals had a hard time living there. But Chery said this kind of tidal zone also had some advantages. After splitting into three groups, the kids acted like marine biologists *and* detectives to find out what these advantages were.

Carl's group figured out what kind of plants and animals lived in different parts of the zone. They laid down a big square called a quadrat. Then they described the land it was on and listed all the living things inside it. That finished, they moved up a dozen feet and took another count.

"Think about the conditions that affect which species can live in each quadrat," said Carl. "How could the substrate, or type of ground, make a difference? How about the area's time above and below water?"

"This substrate is one hundred percent rock," said Greg expertly by the time the kids did their fourth quadrat.

"Eighty-five percent of it is also covered with knotted wrack seaweed, a good protective blanket for animals that need to stay moist and hidden," said Carl, as he lifted up a clump. "Now, let's see who's living here."

While Andrew counted 155 smooth periwinkles in the quadrat, Greg poked between some rocks. "Do dead mussels count?" he asked.

ABOVE: "Be careful, Sedrine," said Carl, "you almost broke the No Falling rule."

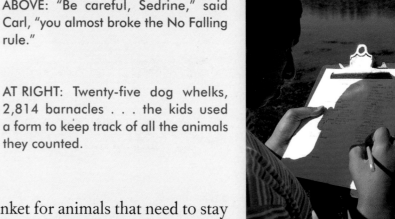

AT RIGHT: Twenty-five dog whelks, 2,814 barnacles . . . the kids used a form to keep track of all the animals they counted.

"Nope, only live ones," said Carl. Then he showed a snail to the group. "Here's a common periwinkle—a big surprise. This animal doesn't usually live this far up the tidal zone. It's dry for too long, with too many changes in temperature and salinity, or saltiness."

"What's this?" asked Bill.

"A ribbon worm," Carl answered, "a predator that fires a harpoonlike part of its body to catch its prey."

"I think I killed it by accident," said Bill.

"Look at the bright side," said Carl, "some tiny clam worm will live longer because of you."

"Ninety-three smooth periwinkles and counting . . ."

Jennifer's group was measuring the beach's slope. Using two poles and math, they mapped the beach's incline from the ocean to the black zone, the top of the tidal zone. They also calculated how high the tide rose and how far it traveled up the shore.

"Why is a beach's slope important to our lifestyle?" asked Kendra.

"I wouldn't want to sunbathe on a very steep one," said Jennifer, "but let's ask that question in terms of the animals living here. The steeper the beach, the harder it's hit by waves. Steep beaches are also usually rocky because waves carry sand away."

"It wouldn't be too good for clams that live in sand," someone commented.

"And animals that do live here must have a way to avoid being tossed by the waves," Carl explained later. "Crabs have claws and hold on to seaweed. Limpets clamp down on rocks so hard that, if you tried to pry one off, your fingernails would break before it lost its grip. Animals like periwinkles crawl into cracks between stones."

Higher up the beach, Carl's group studied their seventh quadrat. "One hundred percent rock and about sixty-five percent covered with bladder wrack seaweed," said Carl. "What's happening to our smooth periwinkle population?"

"It's getting smaller," said Bill.

"I think I see an anemone," said Ben, his face deep in the rocks.

Carl took a look. "It's unusual to see one this high up. Anemones don't have shells that keep in moisture, so they can easily dry out. Up here, they need to be very well protected. This one's in the shade underneath a rock covered by seaweed, a spot as cool and moist as somewhere lower in the tidal zone."

The kids figured out that the beach was 42 meters (136.5 feet) from the water to the high-tide line. Its vertical height was 5.1 meters (16.5 feet).

21

Meanwhile, Chery's group was testing Raccoon Beach's water. They measured how much oxygen, salt, and acid were in it. They even took its temperature.

"All these things help define this environment and who can live here," Chery said. "Take temperature, for example. Many fish that live near Florida don't live here, and temperature is one reason why."

Richard tested the water's pH, its acidity, and came back worried. "Maybe I'm doing something wrong," he said. "I get the same results everywhere I measure."

"I guess these organisms are lucky," said Chery. "If the pH of the sea and tide pools are the same, they don't need to adapt to something new."

The kids found more oxygen in the ocean than in the tide pools. As Richard guessed, "All that wave action stirs oxygen from the air into the ocean."

By the time the kids did their last quadrat, they felt like pros.

"One hundred percent rock substrate," announced Andrew.

"Just bits of wrackweed here and there," said Nicole.

"We're too high up the tidal zone for much to be living here—just some barnacles," said Vlad, who eventually counted fifty of them within the square.

Bill just stared at the corner of the tide pool inside their quadrat. It was filled with rotting seaweed. "Do we have to put our hands in there? That stuff looks like toxic waste!"

"What do you mean *we*, Bill?" Carl joked. Then he said, "We'll just say this tide pool contains so much decomposing seaweed, there's not enough oxygen to support much animal life."

The kids picked their way back across slippery, seaweed-covered rocks. Later, Carl put the day's discoveries into context.

Despite its crashing waves, a place like Raccoon Beach is a more stable environment than the calmer beaches inside the bay. The ocean is much bigger than the bay, so its temperature and salinity don't change as much. Think of a bathtub of seawater and a filled juice glass. Which one would heat up faster in sunshine or cool down more quickly in winter? Which would be more affected by freshwater when it rained?

The kids also learned that fewer species can survive in the top of the tidal zone. The higher up they go, the more they're exposed to land conditions. And if you're basically a sea creature, that's tough. You get rained on with freshwater. You're pelted by the sun's ultraviolet rays. You get dried out.

"I wouldn't mind being dried out," said Roger, whose pants were sopping wet. "I can't wait to get back into the van!"

That night, the kids made a presentation of their discoveries.

THE BLACK ZONE, just below dry land and above the highwater mark, occasionally gets wet from the spray of waves and the highest of high tides. Blue-green bacteria coat its rocks like black paint. A jellylike covering keeps this bacteria from drying out. But it can't save the bacteria from rough periwinkles that scrape it off the rocks for food.

THE UPPER ZONE is only underwater at high tide. Here, barnacles glue themselves to rocks and wait for high tide to bring them food. But these barnacles are food for dog whelks that drill holes into a barnacle's shell or force open its "trap door" with their foot and eat what's inside.

Tidal Zones

The tidal zone has many subzones on its way from dry land to ocean. Each subzone's set of plants and animals is determined by how long they can survive in air and underwater. Some animals, like crabs, travel between different zones. Others, like mussels, may use one zone as a nursery and another to live their adult lives.

THE MIDDLE ZONE is both underwater and exposed to air during every tidal cycle. Here, seaweeds called rockweed and wrackweed use air bladders to stay afloat so they can catch the sunlight when they are in water. At both high tide and low, the seaweed provides cover for animals like mussels, smooth periwinkles, limpets, and this hiding crab.

THE LOWER ZONE is only exposed to air briefly, during low tide. Here, seaweeds like this Irish moss and sea lettuce protect the zone's residents—crabs, these sea urchins, and sea stars—from drying out or being pounded by waves.

THE SUBTIDAL ZONE, always underwater, is home to larger seaweed called kelp. This busy zone is filled with familiar creatures like crabs, sea urchins, sea stars, fish, and lobsters. It is also inhabited by jellyfish, marine worms, anemones, and sea squirts like the sea vase pictured here.

CHAPTER 4

LIFE in a TIDE POOL

E ven at low tide, parts of the tidal zone keep their seawater. These tide pools can be little water-filled caves under rocks or even ponds twenty feet across. They are nature's aquariums, home to a semipermanent community of sea plants and animals.

Under a tide pool's seaweed, a hermit crab trades its outgrown shell for a bigger one. A sea star holds up the light-sensitive tip of its arm to "look" for a dark, safe corner. Water flows in and out of holes in a purple sponge's body, bringing in tiny bits of food.

"People often say, 'Life's a beach,' because they think being on a beach is free and easy," said Chery. "But it's no vacation for the creatures living there. Life can actually be dangerous for animals in a tide pool."

Winter can turn a small tide pool icy cold. The summer sun makes it too hot for comfort. And, as the temperature rises, oxygen bubbles out of the water, leaving less for animals to breathe. A tide pool's water can evaporate, too, making the water that remains much too salty. Rain can make the water not salty enough.

The kids kept all this in mind when they checked out a tide pool. But their real interest was finding animals that lived there. At first glance, a tide pool can look empty or just, as one kid called it, "Seaweed City." But with patience . . .

"Hey," said Bill. "I was feeling around under a rock and this sea urchin pricked me."

Tide pools come in all sizes. Big ones . . .

. . . and others with just a tiny bit of water.

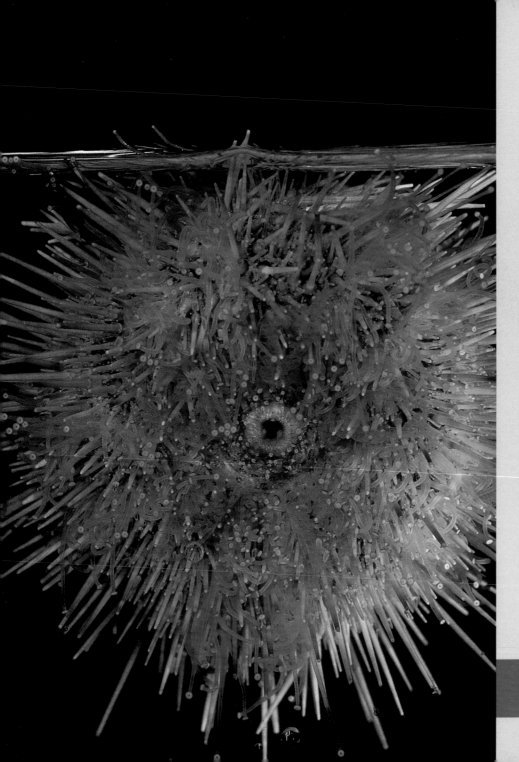

"That sure is a big one," said Chery. "Remember those tube feet sea stars have on their undersides? The urchins have them, too. This one's using its tube feet to hold pieces of shell against its body for camouflage."

"Here's a little starfish," said Vlad, holding up his find.

"That's actually called a blood star," said a counselor named Lila Austin.

"Will it suck my blood?"

"Actually, its name comes from its bright red color," she answered as she examined the tiny sea star. "Look, one of its arms has been eaten off."

"Is it going to die?" Vlad asked.

"Nope," said Lila, "its arms grow back. If one is crushed, the sea star gets rid of it and grows another."

Now scientists know that even one sea star arm can grow four new ones—

Urchins also use their tube feet to move around to graze on algae.

Crabs, like this rock crab, clean up tide pools by feeding on dead and dying prey.

When threatened by an enemy, the sea cucumber hurls its internal organs out its rear and tries to crawl away during the confusion. Within a week or so, it grows new ones. Luckily, Jen C. stroked one without this happening. "It feels like a slimy old carrot that's gotten all soft and floppy," she said.

Dog whelks are the terrors of the tide pool. They hunt mussels, snails, and barnacles.

This anemone may look like a flower, but it's actually a hollow relative of the jellyfish. Its "petals" are a ring of tentacles that first sting its prey, then drag the food toward a mouth in its center.

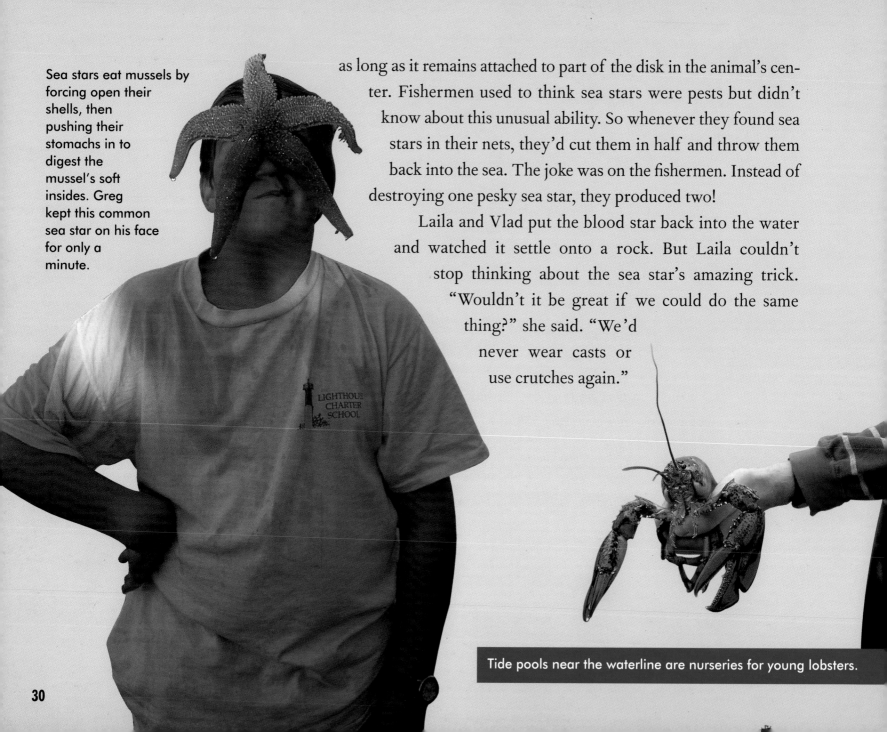

Sea stars eat mussels by forcing open their shells, then pushing their stomachs in to digest the mussel's soft insides. Greg kept this common sea star on his face for only a minute.

as long as it remains attached to part of the disk in the animal's center. Fishermen used to think sea stars were pests but didn't know about this unusual ability. So whenever they found sea stars in their nets, they'd cut them in half and throw them back into the sea. The joke was on the fishermen. Instead of destroying one pesky sea star, they produced two!

Laila and Vlad put the blood star back into the water and watched it settle onto a rock. But Laila couldn't stop thinking about the sea star's amazing trick. "Wouldn't it be great if we could do the same thing?" she said. "We'd never wear casts or use crutches again."

Tide pools near the waterline are nurseries for young lobsters.

Bugged by Bugs

"Mud helps keep them away," said Katelyn, "at least until it dries."

The kids loved whelks and anemones, but they hated other examples of Maine wildlife. Every day, right around sunset, the mosquitoes were out and biting.

"I just load on that stinky repellent," said Alexa. "Mosquitoes don't come near me—but no one else does either."

"Bugs are bothersome," agreed Carl, "that's why they call 'em 'bugs.'"

Carl had a way to keep the kids from being "bugged" all night long. "Run the last ten steps to your cabins so you knock the mosquitoes off before you get inside," he said. "If you don't like them outside, you'll hate them buzzing around your cabin."

Good advice, but it didn't help when the kids were outdoors.

"I wish every mosquito would die," Vlad grumbled as he slapped his neck yet another time.

"Who knows what would happen," said Greg. "Maybe a lot of things that eat them—like bats, birds, and spiders—would die too."

"Stupid food chain," Vlad said. "If we could last, I bet we'd evolve out of the problem in twenty thousand years or so."

MOSQUITO

MAINE'S STATE BIRD

A former camper wrote on a cabin wall: "If bugs were people, this place would be China."

CHAPTER 5

ON the OPEN SEA

After many days exploring the shore, the kids were scheduled to spend a day on the ocean. As they walked toward the boat, some of them were excited about the fish they might catch. Others were nervous about what they might lose.

"Last time I was on a boat, I saw this girl take off her sock and use it to throw up in," said Mary K. "Then she just washed it out in the ocean."

"At least this boat doesn't have a kitchen," said Katelyn. "When you're seasick, the smell of hot dogs makes things a lot worse."

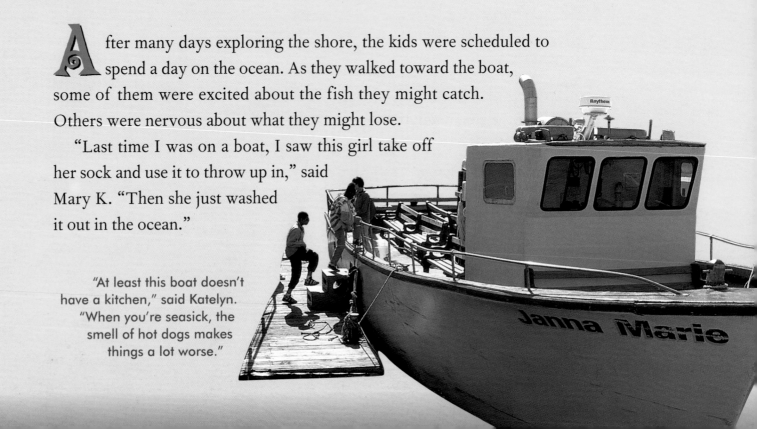

"Not a bad idea," said Bill. "Sometimes when I feel sick, I just throw up and feel better."

Luckily the seas were calm, so the kids didn't have to worry about seasickness. Carl didn't want to worry about kids falling overboard, so he passed out life jackets.

"Do we have to wear these?" asked Greg. "I can swim."

"Not for long in this water," said Carl. "It's very cold, about fifty-five degrees. After a few minutes, your arms and legs wouldn't work so well. But let's not test it out. Today's safety rule: Sit on the rail if you want, but always keep at least one foot flat on the deck."

Carl had to repeat the rule many times once the boat got going. The kids were too busy looking at the ocean to remember their feet.

"If you look down, you can see jellyfish," said Paul.

"I see something shiny in the water," yelled Roger.

"That's a rock," said Andrew.

"No, it's a seal's head!" said Alexa.

"I'm stylin'," said Roger as he put on his life jacket. "I don't know," said Kendra, "we all look like we've just gained fifteen pounds."

Soon the kids saw some animals they recognized right away.

"WHALES!" they cried.

"Those are two fin whales," said Carl. "One looks to be about seventy feet long, the other one sixty-five."

The boat rocked as the kids ran from side to side to find the whales each time they came up for air. Huge creatures, fin whales are second in size only to the blue whale. After taking in several breaths through the two nostrils—or blowholes—on top of their heads, they dove back down to feed. Fin whales often work in pairs to round up and eat schools of small fish or shrimplike animals called krill.

"Here whaley, whaley," Mary K. called out impatiently, waiting for them to resurface.

"That's not going to help," said Jen B.

"Maybe not," Mary K. replied, "but if they come up right beside the boat next time, I'm taking the credit!"

"Are they going all the way down to the bottom of the ocean?" Bill asked the next time they disappeared.

"They could—the ocean is only about four hundred feet deep here," said boat

"Now I've got a lot of pictures of whales' backs," said Rand.

captain Butch Harris, checking an instrument called a fish finder. Then he pointed to a blob of white dots on its computer screen. "There's a school of fish about three hundred feet down," he said. "I bet that's where those whales are going."

Butch followed the feeding whales for a while. Then it was time for the kids to do some fishing of their own. Carl passed out the poles—and some advice.

"Let your lines out slowly so they don't get tangled. Then bob them up and down to

Many cormorants nest on cliffs and ledges by the ocean. Unlike other seabirds that swim and dive for fish, cormorants don't have water-repellent oil on their feathers. They must stretch their wings out to dry.

The kids saw a puffin that nested on a nearby island. Puffins catch small fish called herring to feed their young.

attract the fish. And, Hannah," Carl called out, "keep at least one foot on the deck. If you fall in the water, you'll scare all our fish away."

"I think I caught a fish," cried Rand as she began to reel in her line. When her neighbor's fishing pole started to feel the tug, Carl realized what had really happened.

"Actually, you caught Alexa," he said, helping them untangle their lines.

"I've got one," said Nicole as she reeled in a flopping ten-incher.

"That's a young cod," said Carl. "The law says we can't keep any under nineteen inches, so we'll have to throw this one back."

Sea robins usually live on the ocean bottom, feeding on squid and other fish. Once, a kid caught two on one line—the second sea robin was trying to eat the first and was hauled up along with it.

"How about this thing?" said Paul, pulling in his line.

"That's a sea robin," said Butch. "You can't eat that either."

"Who'd want to?" said Richard. "That's one ugly fish!"

Active tides push nutrients up from the bottom of the sea to make Cobscook Bay a rich feeding ground for fish. Maybe the availability of so much natural food explains why the kids didn't have much luck that afternoon. When it was time to head back, the kids were empty-handed.

"It looks like we'll have to have pizza for dinner," said Carl.

"Thank God," Amie muttered under her breath.

ABOVE: This may be the last time Matt tries sea urchin eggs.

AT LEFT: "We should find everything there is to eat around here and make a big salad," said Bill.

CHAPTER 6

AND OTHER NEAT STUFF

A Different Kind of Seafood

Most of the time, the kids ate foods like tacos and pizza. Occasionally, they were a little more adventurous. On a nature walk, Carl pointed out plants growing in the upper tidal zone that people can eat. The kids sampled one called marsh pickle.

"It does taste like a pickle," said Greg.

"Wicked salty," said Paul.

"This tastes like well-salted spinach," said Carl, holding up a sprig of orache for a brave volunteer.

Chery pointed out a young bald eagle that, when fully grown, will have a brown body with a white head and tail.

Matt tried it. "I don't like spinach that much," he said, "but this is okay." Then he fed the rest to the field station's dog.

Later, at the lab, Carl pulled a sea urchin out of a tank. "Sea urchins used to be so common around here that they carpeted the ocean floor. Then fishermen started catching them because people in Japan like to eat urchin roe. Now you have to search for them."

He cut open a female urchin and picked out her large orange cluster of eggs, or roe. "They eat it raw," he said, holding it out for an even braver volunteer.

Bill gave it a try. "I think it tastes like salmon," he said.

"I think I'll just wait for lunch," said Laila.

Last century, arctic tern feathers were a popular decoration for ladies' hats. These birds were hunted almost to extinction. Today, they stop in this part of Maine on their annual migration all the way to the bottom of the globe.

Wildlife Watch

Even short boat rides turned into wildlife watches. On their way across the bay, the kids spotted many different birds soaring overhead. They saw dolphins glide below the water's surface. They also saw seals poking their heads above water to stare at them.

"When you find a seal," said Carl, "tell the other kids where to look instead of showing them. Pointing fingers look like pointing guns

Unlike other types of seals, harbor seals are great swimmers from birth.

and that makes seals nervous. Many of them have been shot at by fishermen who don't want any competition catching fish."

Aquaculture

Some farmers grow beans and corn, but people who "farm" the sea grow fish. The kids visited a salmon farm where huge pens in the ocean held up to 24,000 fish.

"If I were one of those fish, I would swim down deep and get out," said Sedrine.

"They can't, there's a net floor on the pen," Chery explained. "And a second layer of nets keeps things even safer. A few years ago, a seal chewed his way in to eat his fill. Then most of the fish escaped through the hole he made. Twenty thousand fish, that's an expensive loss for these guys."

It takes about eighteen months for a baby salmon to grow to ten pounds and be ready for market.

The kids watched the pens. Every so often, a salmon would leap into the air.

"Why are they jumping?" asked Kendra.

"Maybe they're having the Salmon Olympics," said Jen C. "This is their high jump."

"Who's doing the judging?" said Laila.

Algae Pressing

"You guys may wonder why we should care about algae," said Jennifer. "But if we didn't have algae to give off the oxygen that we need to breathe, we wouldn't be around ourselves. This group of water plants, which includes seaweed, produces about eighty percent of Earth's oxygen."

The kids gathered seaweed to make an art project, pressing it onto paper the same way you press flowers. When Rand picked up some dulse, Jennifer tore off a piece and began munching.

"You're eating my art project!" said Rand.

"You eat that?" Roger said in amazement.

"You do too, whenever you have Jell-O or pudding or milkshakes from McDonald's," said Jennifer. "Seaweed is used in lots of foods to thicken them and hold them together."

"I'll never eat that stuff again!" said Roger.

"Are you going to stop brushing your teeth, too?" Jennifer replied. "Guess what's in toothpaste!"

The kids arranged their seaweed on paper and pressed it between wooden boards. "It's harder than it looks," said Andrew.

"This stuff isn't as slimy as I thought," said Richard.

OUT with the TIDE

Jen B. and Amie at high tide . . .

On their last day, the kids spent both low and high tide at a part of the bay called Reversing Falls. Here, water rushed in and out so forcefully, it looked like a river with whitewater rapids. The kids were told not to wade in very far; the current was strong enough to carry them away.

In fact, Chery remembered once seeing a moose that got spooked and jumped in. "Moose are huge animals, but we were worried about him," she told the kids. "He went under more than once. We cheered when we finally saw him climb onto the far shore!"

The kids promised to be careful, but nothing could keep them from their final low-tide treasure hunt.

"My feet are already used to the seaweed," said Jen B., clambering barefoot over boulders slick with rockweed. She found a sea star and tickled its tube feet. "I used to think this was nasty, but it's really so cool."

"Yeah," Rand agreed. "At normal camp, all you do is swim."

"I'm coming back next year," said Jen B. "Who knows what I'll find?"

Poking around rocks and looking at tide pools, the kids imagined what it would be like to be marine biologists and study sea life.

The good things: "The ocean, the animals, and the places you get to go."

The bad ones? "The papers you have to write, BUGS, and how far you have to travel from home."

"Wait a minute," said Jennifer. "You could study marine biology right in Boston, where most of you are from."

. . . joined by much of the group at low tide.

"The water is so polluted there," said Bill. "I'd probably be looking at seven-eyed fish and sea stars with forty arms!"

Right before high tide, the kids returned to the shore—what was left of it. In the six hours since low tide, water had swallowed most of the beach. Now safely underwater, the animals of the tidal zone were busy feeding.

Carl had everyone sit on the rocks that remained so they could put their feet in the water and feel the tide turn.

"In exactly three minutes, the water will come to a dead stop. That will be high tide," said Jennifer. "A few minutes later, it will start going out again."

"Sh-h-h," said Carl. "Let's see if you can *hear* the water turn as well."

The kids didn't say a word. They looked across the still waters. They listened to crickets chirping. Matt picked up a sea urchin and felt its sharp spines. Roger found a flat stone and cheated by skipping it across the silent bay.

"Are our feet supposed to be getting numb?" asked Andrew.

"Take them out of the water if you're cold," said Carl, "but think about how lucky it is that you can. When you're cold, you can move your feet or put on a sweater. And since you're warm-blooded, you have an internal thermometer that helps you adjust and keep warm.

"Imagine life as a barnacle or mussel. Imagine being cold-blooded so that your body temperature depended upon the surrounding environment. These animals can be sitting in sixty-degree water and suddenly, when the tide drops, they are hit with an eighty-five-degree day. With the sun pounding on the rocks, it could be hotter than that."

"Listen," Mary H. called excitedly, "I can hear it now!"

The water had started its rush toward the ocean. Within moments, Amie saw her ankle bracelet peek out of the bay. Matt put his sea urchin back in the water and the outgoing current pushed it toward the sea.

The tide's endless cycle had once more begun.

GLOSSARY

ALGAE—plant forms that mostly live in water and range in size from one-celled to giant kelp

BAY—water that is partially surrounded by land and protected from wind and waves

BLOWHOLES—openings on top of whales' and dolphins' heads used for breathing

BYSSAL THREADS—threadlike strands mussels make and use to attach themselves to a solid surface

COLD-BLOODED ANIMAL—an animal without built-in temperature controls whose body temperature is greatly affected by the outside environment

DECOMPOSE—to break down into separate elements, to decay

EVAPORATE—to change into vapor

FILTRATION—the act of separating out little solid pieces from liquid

FISH FINDER—a machine that uses sonar to locate fish underwater

FOOD CHAIN—a series of living things dependent upon one another for food. For example, we eat big fish, which eat little fish, which eat seaweed.

MARINE BIOLOGIST—a person who studies plants and animals that live in or near the sea

pH—the measure of a liquid's acidity or alkalinity

PREDATOR—an animal that hunts other animals

QUADRAT—small, measured plot of land used to study how plants and animals are distributed in an area

RADULA—the filelike tongue of a snail

ROE—the eggs of certain animals

SALINITY—saltiness

SLOPE—a surface that's on an incline

SPECIMEN—an individual or item that represents a whole group

SPECIES—a group of plants or animals with common qualities

SUBSTRATE—the surface upon which an organism grows or is attached

TIDAL ZONE—the land that is covered and uncovered between high and low tides

TIDE POOL—a pool of seawater left on the beach when the tide goes out

TUBE FEET—little fluid-filled body parts on the underside of certain animals that help them move and handle food

VERTICAL FOOT—twelve inches that are measured straight up and down

WARM-BLOODED ANIMAL—an animal that can maintain its own body temperature regardless of the outside environment

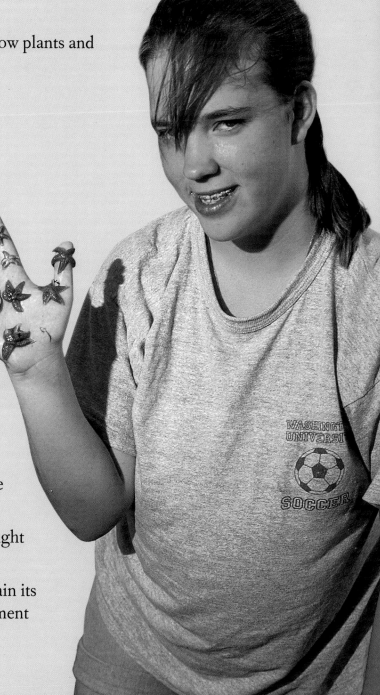

FURTHER READING

Other Nonfiction Books About Tidal Zones and Marine Biology

Davis, Ellen. *Marine Biology*. New York: Thames & Hudson, Inc., 1993.

Malnig, Anita. *Where the Waves Break: Life at the Edge of the Sea*. Minneapolis: Carolrhoda Books, Inc., 1985.

Parker, Steve (Eyewitness Books). *Seashore*. New York: Alfred A. Knopf, 1989.

Silverstein, Alvin, and Virginia Silverstein. *Life in a Tidal Pool*. Boston: Little, Brown and Company, 1990.

Wu, Norbert. *Beneath the Waves: Exploring the Hidden World of the Kelp Forest*. San Francisco: Chronicle Books, 1992.

Novels That Have Marine Biology as a Theme (all available in paperback):

George, Jean Craighead. *Shark Beneath the Reef*. New York: HarperCollins Children's Books, 1989.

L'Engle, Madeleine. *The Arm of the Starfish*. New York: Farrar, Straus, and Giroux, Inc., 1965.

O'Dell, Scott. *Island of the Blue Dolphins*. Boston: Houghton Mifflin, 1960.

For Information About the Marine Science Field Experience, Cosponsored by Boston's Museum of Science and Suffolk University:

MUSEUM OF SCIENCE
SCIENCE PARK
BOSTON, MA 02114-1099
TEL: 617-589-0300 • FAX: 617-589-0474
WEB: www.mos.org